50
Good **IRA** Ideas

Fifty good ideas to make the best use of IRAs, Roth IRAs, 403(b) and Qualified Plans

Version 1.0

Leon C. LaBrecque, JD, CPA, CFP®, CFA

©2015, All rights reserved.

Disclaimer:

This book is intended for informational purposes only. Best efforts were used to ensure that the information contained in this book is accurate; however, the author and every person involved in the creation of this book disclaim any warranty as to the accuracy or completeness of its contents. This book is not a substitute for obtaining legal, financial and other professional advice as the contents of the book apply to your individual situation. It is recommended that you obtain legal, financial and other advice or assistance before acting on any information contained in this book. The writer and every person involved in the creation of this book disclaim any liability arising from contract, negligence, or any other cause of action, to any party, for the book's contents or any consequences arising from its use.

LJPR Financial Advisors
5480 Corporate Drive #100
Troy, MI 48098
ljpr.com

(248) 641-7400

Copyright © 2015 by Leon C. LaBrecque. All rights reserved.
ISBN: 978-1-4951-7306-6

Printed in the United States of America

"It should be called the 50 best IRA ideas. LJPR has hit the ball out of the park, as usual."
    -- Sanford Mall, JD, CELA, CAP, VA Accredited Attorney
       MALL MALISOW & COONEY, PC

"50 Good Ideas really shows how an IRA can be a Swiss Army Knife of planning, be useful for everything from estate tax reduction to college funding to dynasty building. Great ideas in a quick format."
    -- Robert Weins, JD, CPA
       Insights[3]

"What's good about this book is that a professional can use it, or an interested individual can take the ideas and make them work. There's a lot of great ideas summarized in a simple fashion."
    -- Nick Valenti, CLU®, ChFC, CFP® - **President and CEO**
       Michigan Financial Companies

"50 Good IRA Ideas shows the interesting ways you can use IRAs to amplify wealth. Some of the Roth conversion ideas are truly useful."
    -- Bernie Shinkel, PhD
       Alpha Investment Management, Inc.

About the Author
Leon LaBrecque JD, CPA, CFP®, CFA

Leon has specialized in servicing individuals, families, and small businesses in the areas of financial, estate, and tax planning for over 34 years. Leon is the founder and CEO of LJPR Financial Advisors. Under Leon's 26 years of leadership, LJPR has grown to be recognized as one of the top independent investment advisors in the country.

He has a passion for sharing his vast wealth management knowledge with everyone he can. He has authored a number of corporate retirement programs for municipalities and companies across the country including CalPERS, the states of Montana, and Washington, and Fortune 500 clients including General Motors, Ford Motor Company, Lucent, and AT&T, among others. In 1989, Leon founded the Masters of Science in Finance program while serving as the Department Chair of Finance and Economics at Walsh College. LaBrecque's specialties include investment management for foundations and non-profit organizations, financial planning for automotive employees and retirees, and retirement planning for police officers and firefighters.

Leon also helped start the Michigan Alpha Project, for which he personally provided $100,000 for Walsh College investment students to invest in an all-Michigan portfolio.

Leon's passion for the outdoors is as strong as his passion for helping people make educated financial decisions. When he's not advising clients or hashing out the next big thing in wealth management, you'll probably find him with his family kayaking one of our Great Lakes or training his three golden retrievers.

About LJPR Financial Advisors

LJPR Financial Advisors is an independent, fee-only wealth management firm headquartered in Troy, Michigan. The company has been offering comprehensive fiduciary services since 1989. Its team of experienced advisors has a unique way of connecting with clients to help them feel confident, secure and ready for the future. Tax Planning, Financial Planning, Estate Planning, Investment Management all come together to optimize clients' wealth. Detailed Social Security analysis, Monte Carlo simulations, and IRA planning are all components of the company's holistic approach.

Contact Information

Leon C. LaBrecque, JD, CPA, CFP®, CFA

LJPR Financial Advisors
5480 Corporate Drive, #100
Troy, MI 48098
Phone: 248.641.7400
Fax: 248.641.7405
Email: leon.labrecque@ljpr.com
Twitter: @leonlabrecque
www.linkedin.com/in/leonlabrecque

Contents

Idea 1: New rule on 60-day rollovers 5

Idea 2: A good use of the IRA rollover rule 5

Idea 3: New rule on inherited IRAs 6

Idea 4: Protect the kids from the money and the money from the kids 6

Idea 5: Double your IRA firepower if you have after-tax money in a qualified plan 7

Idea 6: Watch out for hard-to-value assets 8

Idea 7: An oldie and goodie, the Qualified Charitable Distribution (QCD) 8

Idea 8: The Kid Roth 9

Idea 9: The Mom Roth 9

Idea 10: Top your bracket 10

Idea 11: The Dynasty Roth 12

Idea 12: The Backdoor Roth 12

Idea 13: The Roth AMT slayer 13

Idea 14: The Roth Mulligan 15

Idea 15: The Serial Roth conversion 15

Idea 16: The Roth estate tax reducer. 17

Idea 17: Use your RMD to pay the taxes on a Roth Conversion 18

Idea 18: Always pay taxes on conversions out of other non-IRA funds 18

Idea 19: When to take a spousal rollover and when not to 19

Idea 20: Age 70 ½ and the first Required Minimum Distribution 20

Idea 21: RMDs in-kind after age 70 ½ 20

Idea 22: Take your RMD at the end of the year 21

Idea 23: Only take the RMD 22

Idea 24: Watch state tax laws on distributions and conversions 22

Idea 25: Use the Substantially Equal Periodic Payments (SEPP) exemption to avoid the 10% early withdrawal penalty 23

Idea 26: Use a Qualified Plan or 403(b) to dodge RMDs 24

Idea 27: Use an IRA rollover to avoid 20% withholding on a Qualified Plan distribution 24

Idea 28: Make Roth contributions after age 70 ½ 25

Idea 29: Use the age 55 exemption from a Qualified Plan 26

Idea 30: Use the age 50 exemption if you are a police officer or firefighter 26

Idea 31: Pay management fees on a regular IRA out of the IRA 27

Idea 32: Buy actual Real Estate in your IRA 27

Idea 33: Deduct the loss on your Roth 29

Idea 34: The QLAC 29

Idea 35: Filing a 5329 to set the statute of limitations 30

Idea 36: Mind your beneficiaries 31

Idea 37: How to write a good beneficiary designation 31

Idea 38: Leave your Traditional IRA to charity 32

Idea 39: Leave your IRA to a Charitable Remainder Trust 32

Idea 40: Leave your IRA to a Charitable Gift Annuity 33

Idea 41: Don't leave your Roth to charity 33

Idea 42: Don't try to convert an inherited IRA to a Roth 34

Idea 43: Title your Inherited IRA correctly 34

Idea 44: Stretch the benefit of the Inherited IRA 34

Idea 45: Asset protection tip, don't comingle rollovers and Traditional IRAs 35

Idea 46: Use an IRA to get special withdrawal treatments if under 59 ½ 35

Idea 47: Roll over a Designated Roth Account (DRAC) to a Roth IRA 35

Idea 48: If you name a trust as a beneficiary, make sure it has a see-through provision 36

Idea 49: Use your Roth IRA as a college education savings tool...........36

Idea 50: Use your Roth IRA as an emergency fund account 38

Conclusion 38

The world of Individual Retirement Plans and Qualified Plans (in which I'll include 401(k) and §403(b) plans) is an area where there is vast opportunity and vast complexity. I've compiled a list of planning ideas and opportunities in the area. I also recommend the materials of Natalie Choate, Michael Kitces and Ed Slott. Natalie's book, *Life and Death Planning for Retirement Benefits*, is a must read for tax wonks like me. Michael Kitces' website, kitces.com, has the *"Nerd's eye view"* of articles and education in Financial Planning. From one nerd to another, I like Mike. And Ed Slott's *"2015 Retirement Decisions Guide"* is a great read on IRA Advice. Ed is the dean of planners. For everyone else, I hope the 50 ideas below are useful. Note the icons next to the topics. Some ideas may cover more than one topic, and will have multiple icons. You'll probably read these out of order (I call this a 'bathroom book'). I think you will find at least some of the ideas useful. Obviously, if you need help with an idea, reach out to us at info@ljpr.com or my personal e-mail at leon.labrecque@ljpr.com. Thanks for reading.

New Stuff for 2015:

Idea 1: New rule on 60-day rollovers. There is a new rule from the Tax Court case of *Bobrow* which now allows only one 60-day rollover per year[1]. Prior to this case, you could take a distribution from an IRA in your name (not taking withholdings), use the money for something and roll it back into the IRA within 60 days with no tax. You could do this with different IRAs, allowing you to effectively get a series of tax-free loans from your IRAs. The IRS even indicated, in Publication 590, that you could do a 60-day rollover from each IRA separately. The Tax Court disagreed with this position and has ruled that you may now only take one 60-day rollover from all your IRAs in any 12-month period. If you do decide to take a rollover (where you use the money), do it only once from all of your IRAs within the 12 months.

Idea 2: A good use of the IRA rollover rule. Despite the restriction on multiple rollovers from multiple IRAs, here's a good use of the rule. IRA distributions may have income tax withholding. If taxes are withheld from an IRA distribution, they are deemed to be equally withheld throughout the year. This can be of great benefit if estimates are underpaid.

Leon's example. Suppose Leon owes $80,000 more in taxes than he has paid estimates on. He has the money in the bank, but missed two estimated payments. He will be penalized for underpayment if he catches up on the third estimate. Instead, he takes an $80,000 distribution from his IRA and withholds 100%. Within 60 days, he rolls $80,000 from his bank account back into the IRA. The 60-day rule does take into account tax withholding, so the only rule is that if $80,000 comes out, $80,000 has to go back in. End result? $80,000 of withholding, deemed to have been made on a timely basis.

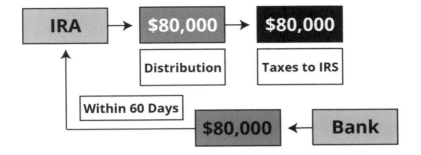

 Idea 3: New Rule on Inherited IRAs. In 2014, the Supreme Court made a landmark decision in the case of *Clark v. Rameker*[2]. The Court held that inherited IRAs were not subject to the asset protection of a regular IRA or spousal IRA. In this case, the daughter of an IRA owner inherited her mom's IRA. The daughter ran into business trouble with her husband and they declared bankruptcy. The creditors went after the IRA. The Supreme Court ruled that the IRA was subject to the claims of creditors. So now, we not only have to worry about the kids blowing our IRA or the IRS getting too much tax, but the creditors of the kids (and possibly the spouse of the kids) getting the IRA. Fortunately, there's a solution (see idea 4).

 Idea 4: Protect the kids from the money and the money from the kids. Given the far-reaching implications of the Supreme Court case, *Clark v. Rameker*, we think inherited IRAs should be protected. The first protection is to keep the kids from taking too much out too fast and paying too much in taxes. With an inherited IRA, if you do it right, the money can be distributed over the life expectancy of the beneficiary. So if Tom dies and leaves his IRA to an infant, she can crawl over to Table I[3] and see that her life expectancy is 82.4 years and take her IRA distributions over 82 years! However, I said she could, not would. The IRA rules state that the minimum amount is over the life

expectancy of the beneficiary. The beneficiary can take funds sooner, anytime they want.

So one thing we want is some way to mandate that the beneficiary take the required minimum amount only, unless there's a good reason. We can do this through an IRA conduit trust. This type of trust takes the required minimum distribution and distributes it to the beneficiary. An independent trustee can distribute more to the beneficiary if the trustee sees fit.

So the conduit protects the IRA from the kids taking too much out, but what about creditors? A well-constructed IRA trust will have a spendthrift clause to protect the assets of the IRA. This clause will keep creditors away from the IRA balance. If the trust provides that the distribution is made to the beneficiary, the beneficiary can obviously collect on the distribution, but the spendthrift clause keeps the creditors at bay.

IRA trusts should be done on a per-account basis. Each kid should have either their own trust or a sub trust which is part of the main IRA trust. I use a sub trust for my kids. There is another kind of IRA trust, called a 'toggle' trust. Here, the trustee can take the distribution into the trust and either give it to the beneficiary or retain it in the IRA trust. This might be used when the child or grandchild has credit or personal problems. Lots of complexity and tax issues here. In all cases, use a separate IRA trust rather than a revocable living trust, and in the case of a 'toggle' trust, use an expert to draft the trust language.

 Idea 5: Double your IRA firepower if you have after-tax money in a qualified plan. There's a new rule, IRS Notice 2014-54[4], that tells us how to handle after-tax contributions in a qualified plan. Who has after-tax contributions? Well, Ford (SSIP) and GM (SSPP) salaried employees have been able to make after tax contributions to their 401(k) plans for years. Many municipalities have after-tax contributions to their pensions for police and firefighter annuity withdrawal. This new rule says you can roll over the taxable portion to a regular IRA and rollover the after-tax

portion directly to a Roth IRA. This is a fabulous planning opportunity, since it takes the taxable monies, defers tax on them, and takes the after-tax monies, puts them in a tax-free Roth. This means that you need to direct the plan to have two rollovers: One to the conventional Rollover IRA and one to your Roth.

 Idea 6: Watch out for hard-to-value assets. The forms used by the IRS to indicate IRA assets and distributions (Form 5498 and Form 1099-R) now have a new box for certain assets, like real estate (see Idea 32) or under-traded securities, like limited partnerships. Be careful when using those assets in an IRA and consider whether holding them is worth IRS scrutiny. The problem lies in valuation. Suppose I have a non-traded REIT in my IRA. I bought it for $50,000 and my broker shows it as worth that. In reality, it is only worth $28,000. Now I attain age 70 ½ and need to take a $50,000 Required Minimum Distribution (RMD). I take the REIT as my distribution (you can take RMDs in kind, see Idea 21). The IRS audits me (because the new Form 1099-R requires the custodian to tell the IRS that I took a hard-to-value asset distribution) and determines that my distribution was too small. I get fined 50% on the portion I failed to take as an RMD (50% of the $22,000). A suggestion is to sell those assets, unless they are a critical part of your IRA and you intend to potentially take it to the mat.

 Idea 7: An oldie and goodie, the Qualified Charitable Distribution (QCD). This is a good one, which has been on-again and off-again by the year-end whims of Congress. If you are over age 70 ½ and taking RMDs, you can give your RMD directly to a qualified charity. This is great from a tax standpoint because you don't include any portion of the QCD in your income. This may keep your social security benefits less taxable (because the taxability of your social security benefit is based on your Modified Adjusted Gross Income (MAGI) and the QCD is not included in MAGI[5]). It may also lower other income characteristics, like the phase-out of personal exemptions and

itemized deductions. You can contribute up to $100,000 per year out of the RMD. It reduces gross income for federal and almost every state income tax. Charitable contributions made from an RMD, must be payable directly to the charity (ies)[6]: No Donor Advised Fund or charitable trust. Keep an eye on the law to make sure it stays in place.

Idea 8: The Kid Roth. Roth IRAs have tax-free growth. The power of compound interest is amazing and the power of tax-free compounding is more amazing. The longer you have a Roth, the better it gets. Suppose a 16-year-old child has a summer or part-time job and earns over $5,500 for the year. Suppose the child does this through college until age 22. During that time, Mom or Dad (or maybe Grandma or Grandpa) deposit $5,500 in a Roth for said youngster, putting it in an index fund. For purposes of my example, let's say they put it in at the beginning of the year. Suppose the investment makes 7.5% annually. By the time the kid reaches 22, the Roth would contain about $52,000. If we left that alone until the kid was 65, the Roth would be worth over $1,164,000, all from seven $5,500 contributions. Did I mention that's $1,164,000 tax-free? But, what if we could instill in said child the notion of saving for retirement and encourage the kid to keep making their own Roth contributions until age 65. Even if the limits on contributions never changed, the kid would have $2,884,000 at 65. If (s) he took out 4%, that's over $115,000 a year tax-free. Of course, we have to get the kid to not touch the Roth. That is a parenting issue, not a money issue, and out of my pay grade.

Idea 9: The Mom Roth. Roth IRAs work best when the deposits are from a low tax bracket and withdrawals are from a high bracket. So, here's a use for a Roth conversion where an IRA holder (like a parent) is in a low bracket and the beneficiary is in a high one. My client's mother was in her 80s and in a nursing home, with significant long-term care expenses. She had a conventional IRA and was taking RMDs. Her tax bracket was effectively zero. All her children were paying taxes. We

converted her Roth in two steps, both gearing to get her into the 10% bracket. The end result was essentially a tax-free Roth and no more RMDs. In this case we had enough money outside the Roth to pay for the mother's care. Otherwise, Mom could have been penalized if she withdrew from the Roth within 5 years of the conversion. This is a good example of a low bracket taxpayer (mom) converting for the benefit of a higher bracket beneficiary.

 Idea 10: Top your bracket. Roth conversions are best when the conversion is made in a lower bracket. A lot of folks don't understand that if they have an IRA, they will probably be in a higher bracket at some point. The reasons include:

- The simple mechanics of RMD calculations. The RMD calculation is a fraction where the numerator is the IRA balance at the end of the previous year and the denominator is the life expectancy from an IRS table. It should be obvious that your life expectancy gets shorter as we age (Note: My favorite IRS quote out of Publication 590[7] is 'when you die, your life expectancy is zero'). Quite simply, this means an IRA distribution will get bigger and can get considerably large, if the IRA investment earns a return greater than the distribution. Simply put, IRA distributions will generally increase and must be taken at age 70 ½.
- The simple mechanics of spousal mortality. Many IRA owners are married and the IRA constitutes a portion of the couple's retirement wealth. Barring some mutual tragedy, one spouse will die first, leaving the IRA to the other. The survivor will likely file as a single person, which is a higher bracket.

So, knowing this, we can project your RMDs and your tax bracket. For people under age 70 ½ and over age 59 ½ who don't need the money, each year we like to convert an amount high enough to 'top off' the tax bracket. Here's an example: Suppose Helen and Joel are under age 70 ½, have a significant IRA ($1M), collect a couple of pensions and two Social Security benefits. Their adjusted gross income without any IRA withdrawals, is $70,000. This includes the taxable portion of their

Social Security benefits. They are squarely in the 15% tax bracket. We'd point out to them that their RMD will probably be over $40,000, which will take them into the 25% bracket. We'd suggest moving some of the IRA into a Roth at the lower 15% rate. How much? Well, it depends on everyone's individual circumstances. In this case they could convert about $25,500 if they used the standard deduction ($70,000, minus $12,600 standard deduction and two $4,000 personal exemptions, is $95,500 of AGI to be at the upper level, $74,900, of the 15% bracket for 2015). This would cost them about $3,825 in federal taxes (they may pay state taxes too, depending on their state). They clearly should pay the taxes on conversion from non-IRA sources.

The ideal bracket top is a younger retiree who doesn't need the money, possibly before collecting Social Security. We like to extensively analyze Social Security taking strategies (meaning deciding when to actually take the benefit) and find that delaying collecting benefits (e.g., to age 70) can be a lucrative strategy. For someone temporarily in a lower bracket or for someone who can control their income, the bracket topping can be very valuable. Here's an example: Crassius and Evita are 62. They sold their business and have ample assets to live on, which are primarily invested in municipal bonds and dividend paying stocks. They have analyzed their Social security taking strategy and have determined that the best approach is to have Crassius file and suspend at age 66 and delay his benefit until age 70, while Evita is collecting 50% of Crassius' benefit. Their adjusted gross income is, for now, until Evita attains age 66, about $40,000, of which all is qualified dividends (they also receive $50,000 of municipal bond interest). Right now, their tax rate is effectively zero, since the dividend tax rate for taxpayers in the 15% bracket is zero and municipal bonds are exempt from income taxes. They can likely convert about $55,500 into a Roth. This will cost them only $4,238 in federal taxes and still keep their dividends tax-free. They can do this each year for at least 4 years and slightly modify the strategy. When Evita reaches age 66 and starts collecting half of Crassius' Social Security, they would have Roth IRAs worth (at 7.5% growth), about $580,000, having only paid about $34,000 of federal taxes.

Idea 11: The Dynasty Roth. Who wouldn't want a dynasty? This idea is actually pretty simple: Create a Roth, either by contributions or conversions, invest it for the very long run, leave it to your spouse and then leave it to a next generation, like grandchildren via an IRA trust (see Idea 4). Let's continue the example from Idea 10 of Crassius and Evita. Let's suppose that they converted $55,000 a year for the 8 years until they were age 70 (and turning 70 ½). This turned into about $580,000, which cost them about $34,000 in federal taxes on the conversion. They leave the Roth alone. For our purposes, suppose that the Roth is in Crassius' name. Crassius lives until age 85 and leaves it to Evita under a spousal rollover. She lives until age 90 and leaves it to the twin grandchildren, Sacco and Vanzetti, in two IRA sub-trusts that allow them the RMD until age 65. The boys are age 18 on Evita's death. Let's see what happens:

- On Crassius' death, his Roth is worth about $1,716,000. Evita rolls it to her spousal Roth rollover. This is tax-free.
- Evita dies five years later and the Roth is worth $2,462,000, which she leaves in an IRA trust to the twin grandsons.
- The grandsons begin receiving their RMD from grandmother's Roth. The distribution starts at around $19,000, but goes up every year, since their life expectancy is 65 years.
- By the time they are 65, they will have Roth IRAs worth $11.4 million each, plus will have tax-free distributions of about $620,000 a year. Over their collection period, they will have received over $8.3 million in distributions and have an $11.4 million balance, which adds up to about $19.7 million each.

Not bad for $34,000 of tax. I'll call that a Dynasty.

Idea 12: The Backdoor Roth. Here is one I use for myself. Contributory Roth IRAs have an income limit (for married couple filing jointly, $183,000 - $193,000; single, $116,000 - $131,000, etc.[8]). Nondeductible IRAs do not.

Roth conversions have no income limit. So I make a contribution to my nondeductible IRA, and convert it to a Roth a few days later with no tax effect. Voila! I have a Roth.

Some important points: First, note that this is a conversion, not a contribution. So conversion rules apply. Also, make sure you file a Form 8606[9] and a Form 5329[10] correctly on your tax return. Second, and this is important; to make this conversion tax-free, you should not have any other IRAs. When you convert an IRA to a Roth, all IRAs are aggregated. So if you only have a nondeductible IRA with $6,500 of after-tax contributions in it and no other IRA assets, that conversion is wholly tax-free. However, if you have $6,500 of nondeductible after-tax contributions in your nondeductible IRA and $58,500 of taxable funds in a Rollover IRA, you will have a taxable conversion for 90% of the nondeductible, even though you only converted the nondeductible IRA. Ed Slott calls this the 'cream in the coffee' rule: You can't get the cream (the taxable part) out of the coffee. You can make this work if you participate in a 401(k) or 403(b) by rolling your Rollover IRA into your 401(k), which will leave you with only nondeductible IRAs. Then you can have a Roth IRA.

Idea 13: The Roth AMT slayer. Here's an interesting and esoteric idea that is kind of like Idea 16 (The Roth estate tax reducer): Use a Roth conversion to reduce Alternative Minimum Tax (AMT). AMT is a frustrating and cumbersome tax imposed on many taxpayers. By its name, AMT is misleading; this tax is neither 'Alternative' nor 'Minimum'. Since you pay the greater of the AMT or regular computed tax, by adding back certain tax-preference items, like discounts on certain stock options, taxes paid to states or for real estate, and even too may exemptions, AMT should probably be named the Mandatory Maximum Tax.

In addition, tax planning with AMT focuses on increasing your taxable income to get rid of the AMT, rather than decreasing your income. The Roth AMT Slayer raises income to get rid of AMT. Note: I would only use this when the taxpayer is in a high bracket and will remain in a high bracket. [By the way, that is one of my favorite blessings to bestow upon you: 'May you always be in the highest tax bracket and be subject to federal estate taxes!'].

To understand the Roth AMT slayer, let's do an example: Guido and Esmeralda are in their early 60s and live in Michigan (because Michigan is a nice state with good college football). They have $350,000 of income in 2014. Guido exercised 200 Incentive Stock Options (ISOs) at $10 per share, when the stock was worth $50 a share. They have significant 401(k) and IRAs. They pay property taxes and state income taxes (about $28,250). They will have high income into the foreseeable future.

	No Roth	Roth conversion ($344,290)
Income (AGI)	350,000	694,290
Itemized deductions	43,850	43,850
Phased out	34,800	32,173
Personal Exemptions	5,056	0
Taxable Income	302,443	662,117
Regular Tax	75,711	208,951
AMT	31,946	0
Total Tax	107,657	208,951
Marginal rate		29.42%

In the above example, adding the $344,290 Roth conversion increased tax by $101,294, or only 29.42%, because the conversion hit the AMT 28% 'sweet spot'. Had they converted in a year where they were not subject to AMT, the tax on that size conversion would have been more like $128,990, or 37.47%. They saved over $27,000 of tax by getting rid of the AMT. Now note that there are other ways to change AMT (like exercising those options before one year), but the purpose of the idea is to show that sometimes AMT can provide an opportunity.

Idea 14: The Roth Mulligan. A Mulligan is a golf idea (invented by a French-Canadian, naturally) in which you get to redo a shot (once a round) if you mess it up. This notion translates to Roth IRAs as a recharacterization. What a recharacterization does is reverse a Roth conversion. Thus, you can do a Roth conversion, then change your mind and recharacterize the transaction by a certain deadline[11]. The transaction will be (in the IRS's terms) as if it had never taken place. This is good news from a tax planning standpoint as well as investment planning. If you did a Roth conversion and your income went up, you could recharacterize and send the Roth back to the Traditional IRA. From an investment standpoint, if you did a Roth conversion and the investment declined, you could recharacterize and then re-convert later (more on that in a moment). You can use the recharacterization as a useful planning tool, like indicated in Idea 15.

Idea 15: The Serial Roth Conversion. This idea takes two Roth characteristics and combines them. Roth conversions can be made in-kind. This means you can take an investment from a Traditional IRA and move it to a Roth. The second point utilizes the recharacterization feature described in Idea 14. Putting these two together, you could have multiple Roth IRAs in a conversion and recharacterize the losers and keep the winners. Using the recharacterization rules, you have until October 15 of the year following the conversion to decide which Roth you want to keep tax-free and which one you want to send back to its taxable origin. To make a simple example, suppose I have two mutual funds I want to use in a conversion: A US stock fund and a European stock fund. I set up two Roth IRAs and put the US fund in one and the European fund in the other.

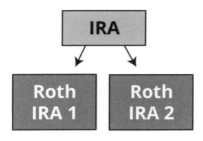

The only probable outcomes (by October 15 of the year after my conversion) are:

- Both investments go up, in which case you keep both and consolidate them into one Roth;
- Both investments go down, in which case you recharacterize (see Idea 14) them both and try again;
- One goes up and the other goes down. Here you keep the winner in the Roth and send the loser back to the taxable IRA by recharacterizing it.

You can do this with any IRA investment, so you could send Apple stock to one Roth and Google stock to another. You could get carried away and have a whole portfolio set up into separate Roth IRAs. I always convert in kind and use a separate Roth until the recharacterization period is over. Why not keep a tax break?

By the way, you don't have to convert in kind to do a serial Roth. You could convert in cash into multiple Roth IRAs and buy different investments. One idea I've heard of is to set up a conversion, split it in half and put one-half in a long (buy) position and the other half in a short (sell) position. Here you might buy an S&P 500 call in one Roth and an S&P 500 put in another Roth. Theoretically, you keep the winner and recharacterize the loser. You then supposedly have a tax free hedge fund. However, this option strategy is return-neutral, so you aren't actually capturing any gain and you have the transaction costs of the trade. I think a better play with multiple Roth IRAs is to use either individual stocks, or funds. I also think that this strategy is the best when you stick with investments you already like. That way, you still have them, either in your converted Roth or back in your Traditional IRA.

Idea 16: The Roth estate tax reducer. We've used this idea a few times. If you have a taxable estate (for 2015, figure approximately 40% of everything above $5.43M for single tax filers, or $10.86M for joint tax filers), converting a conventional IRA (Traditional, Rollover, SEP) will reduce the overall estate tax. It may seem counter-intuitive, but pre-tax IRAs would be double taxed to filers that are exposed to estate tax; once at the estate tax level, and again when the beneficiaries of the retirement account take distributions after inheriting the account. By converting to a Roth IRA, the owner will pay income taxes on the conversion which will reduce the amount of the estate that would be subject to estate tax upon the owner's death. Here's an example: Janet has a taxable estate and is single. She is 77 years old, and will probably live to age 85. She has $10M of assets, $2M of which is in a Traditional (Rollover) IRA. Let's assume her IRA will grow at 7%, less the RMDs (Required Minimum Distributions) which will go away if she converts the entire IRA to a Roth IRA. Let's also assume her non-IRA assets grow at a rate of 3%. She is taking RMDs on her IRA of about $95,000 a year, which are getting bigger because of the RMD rules. For Janet, doing a conversion will reduce the estate taxes by the income taxes paid on the Roth conversion, and the family will enjoy tax-free growth and distributions from the Roth upon inheriting the account. Here's what it looks like:

	No Roth Conversion		
Age 77	IRA	Other	Total
(pre-conversion)	2,000,000	8,000,000	10,000,000
Age 85			
(reinv RMD)	2,181,173	11,183,439	13,365,412
Estate tax			2,801,320
Income Tax	872,789		
IRD ded.*	(349,115)		
Net			**10,040,418**

	Roth Conversion		
Age 77	**Roth IRA**	**Other**	**Total**
(post-conversion)	2,000,000	7,200,000	9,200,000
Age 85			
(reinv RMD)	3,436,372	9,394,366	12,830,739
Estate tax			2,587,451
Income Tax			
IRD ded.*			
Net			**10,243,287**

* This is a deduction for "Income with Respect to a Decedent". It is an income tax deduction for the estate taxes paid on the prospective income taxes. Not all taxpayers can use the IRD deduction, and yes, it's complicated.

Bottom line for Janet's family is a net saving of at least $200,000 in total taxes, not counting the advantage of tax-free income to the kids or other beneficiaries.

Idea 17: Use your RMD to pay the taxes on a Roth Conversion. This is a simple idea for people who have unwanted RMDs (unwanted as in they don't need the money). So the idea basically is to take the amount of the RMD and fully withhold on it, converting the appropriate amount to a Roth to use up all of the tax, or the RMD. So if I am in the 25% bracket, my RMD was $18,000, I would withhold $18,000 in tax and convert $54,000. My IRA would be reduced by the RMD of $18,000 and the $54,000 Roth conversion, total $72,000. 25% tax is $18,000, or the RMD.

Idea 18: Always pay taxes on conversions out of other non-IRA funds. This one is easy. When you make a Roth conversion, or convert Traditional taxable IRA funds into a tax-free Roth, you have to pay taxes on the conversion. The math is quite simple: You should always pay the taxes out of non-IRA funds to maximize the conversion.

Otherwise, the Roth becomes very similar to the IRA you transferred from, because you effectively made a distribution and Roth contribution of the after tax distribution. Pay the taxes from somewhere else, but not the IRA.

Idea 19: When to take a spousal rollover and when not to. When you die, if your spouse is named as your primary beneficiary, your spouse can roll your IRA into their IRA as a spousal rollover[12]. The spousal rollover is a good idea in many cases. The spouse treats the IRA as their own, so they can start taking their RMDs when they reach age 70 ½. For a younger surviving spouse, this can be a big advantage, since they don't have to take the distribution until they reach 70 ½. Suppose Julie, age 60, survives Henry, age 72. Julie can roll Henry's IRA to hers and is not required to take distributions until she reaches age 70 ½. When she does take her RMDs, she uses a more favorable life expectancy table to compute the distributions. If the IRA were worth $500,000 and she made 7%, the IRA would be worth about $1.2M at her reaching age 70 ½. She would then take it out using the RMD table, which would let her take an RMD of about $31,000. If Henry left his IRA to a 60-year-old non-spouse, that person would have to begin to take distributions immediately and use their own life expectancy table. Higher accumulations are available with a spousal rollover.

However, a spouse may not want to use the spousal rollover when the surviving spouse is under 59 ½: If the surviving spouse is under 59 ½ and needs the money, the exemption to the 10% penalty (for under age 59 ½) for distribution upon death is better than the distribution options available under a spousal rollover. However, the surviving spouse may have to take a Required Minimum Distribution of their own, and their options upon the spouse's death are limited.

Another situation might be when the surviving spouse is much older than the decedent: Suppose in my example above, Julie had died before Henry. Henry may be better off leaving Julie's plan alone and taking her RMD when she would have attained the age of 70 ½. This is because a surviving spouse can take distribution on the required beginning date of the deceased person[13], which is typically September 30 of the year after the year the deceased died.

Roth IRAs are not subject to RMD rules and as such, allow additional tax-free growth by using the spousal rollover (See Idea 11).

Last point is that inherited IRAs are subject to the claims of creditors and spousal Rollover IRAs are not. If there is an asset protection issue, the spousal IRA affords more protection.

Idea 20: Age 70 ½ and the first Required Minimum Distribution. For perplexing reasons, the first Required Minimum Distribution must take place by the April 1st of the year following the year you turn age 70 ½[14]. So if Maurice turns 70 ½ on June 12, 2015, he could take his first RMD during 2015, or wait until April 1 of 2016. But if he does that, he will have to take an RMD for both 2015 and 2016 in the 2016 tax year. Normally, taking two distributions in a tax year would have double the tax liability. However, certain times, it might make sense. For instance, if taking the RMD in the first possible year (2015 in my example above) would cause Social Security benefits to be taxable, or if there was some other income in that year. Note that the timing to take the first year RMD gives an opportunity to do some tax planning.

Idea 21: RMDs in-kind after age 70 ½. If you are taking RMDs, you can take distributions in kind. The distribution comes out at fair market value and that is the basis of the distributed asset. So if you had XYZ fund or stock in your IRA and you wanted to keep it, you could take it as a distribution. You'd save the commission or costs, plus you may want XYZ because you think it has appreciation potential. It also stops you from selecting investments you may not want to sell and allows you take the subsequent appreciation as capital gains.

Idea 22: Take your RMD at the end of the year. Once you are subject to RMD, you can take them any time during the year. You must take them, or be subject to a 50% penalty. So the question arises: When is the best time to take the RMD? The market has an upward bias, so we ran a hypothetical case with real numbers. We took an IRA with 60% in the Vanguard S&P 500 index fund and 40% in the Vanguard Total bond Index. We used the current Table III[15] chart (note that in our example, this chart was only used for distributions in 2003 or after) and the real returns from 1994-2014, presuming that the IRA holder was 70 ½ at the beginning. There are studies that show the timing of deposits or withdrawals diminishes over time, so we weren't sure what to expect. Here are the results, assuming you started 20 years ago in a 60% equity/40% bond portfolio:

	Beginning of yr Withdrawal	End of yr Withdrawal	Monthly Withdrawal
Total RMDs	$1,938,091	$1,861,474	$1,881,979
Ending Balance 20 yr	$1,589,294	$1,850,543	$1,731,125
Total	$3,527,385	$3,713,017	$3,613,104

Conclusion? The end of year RMD withdrawal produced less taxable RMDs and left a higher balance than the other two options. In total, using the same investments and calculations, the end of year withdrawal produced a total wealth increased by $185,632 and a balance that was $261,249 bigger. In that period, the option of making an RMD withdrawal at the end of the year created less taxes and produced a higher balance.

Would we always take the RMD at the end of the year? Of course not. If you need the RMD, you'd be better taking it monthly. If you had a designated use for the RMD, like an annual family vacation, or gifts to grandchildren, take it associated with the cash flow. If you had some terminal illness and death looked probable, the RMD would be better off taken before death to help the beneficiaries. Similarly, if the IRA owner were in a low tax bracket and the beneficiaries were in a higher bracket, taking the RMD and possibly bracket topping with a Roth (see Idea 10) would be something to consider.

Idea 23: Only take the RMD. The RMD calculation is based on a joint life expectancy table of an owner and someone ten years older. The way the calculation works is that you take the previous year-end IRA balance and divide that amount by your life expectancy from the IRS table based on your age at year end. So the table indicates the life expectancy at age 71 is 26.5 years. If your 70 ½ birthday was 06/12/15 and you had an IRA balance on 12/31/14 of $500,000, your RMD would be about $18,868 ($500,000/26.5). Note that if your beneficiary was younger by more than 10 years, you would use a different table that would establish a smaller RMD. The RMD table pretty much makes it so the IRA cannot run out of money (theoretically it could if the IRA investments went to zero in a year). Taking only the RMD assures that you should always have some distributions from the IRA and the tax bite from the IRA is as small as it can be. This follows the basic idea of keeping the IRAs (and Roth IRAs for that matter) alive as long as possible.

Idea 24: Watch state tax laws on distributions and conversions. Here's an idea a lot of folks tend to forget, especially on Roth conversions. You pay federal tax on distributions, including conversions to Roth IRAs. You also will probably pay state tax on the conversion. State tax rates vary from the wonderful rate of zero (Alaska, Florida, Nevada, South Dakota, Washington State, Wyoming and Texas) to some pretty high rates, like 10.55% in California or 8.97% in New York, in 2015. In addition, many states have exclusions for certain part of distributions. For people who may have residences in multiple states, like Florida and New York, changing residence before significant withdrawals or conversions can make a big difference. This is particularly true in cases where a large conversion is anticipated, like for estate tax purposes.

Idea 25: Use the Substantially Equal Periodic Payments (SEPP) exemption to avoid the 10% early withdrawal penalty.
IRAs are subject to the rule that funds must remain in the IRA until age 59 ½. There are a variety of exceptions to this rule, including some exceptions only appropriate for IRAs (See Idea 46 for example). One significant exception is the Substantially Equal Periodic Payment (SEPP), or §72(t) exemption. This provides that you may withdraw from an IRA at any age provided you take a series of substantially equal payments over a period associated with your life expectancy. The series of payments cannot be modified for a period of the longer of the time period in which you attain age 59 ½ or 5 years. So if you begin a SEPP at age 52, you must continue it to age 59 ½. If you begin a SEPP at age 57, you must continue it until age 62 (5 years). There are three methods of taking the SEPP:

- You may use your life expectancy under the IRS Single Life Expectancy Table. You take the distribution similar to the calculation of an RMD: You divide the balance in the IRA by your life expectancy. Each subsequent year, subtract one year from the life expectancy. For example, if you were 53, you would take the IRA balance and divide it by 31.4. If the IRA were worth $500,000, your SEPP would be $15,924.
- You may use the life expectancy table and the §7520 rate[16] to determine an amortized distribution. If the interest rate for calculation was 2.04%, the amortization method would produce a SEPP for a $500,000 IRA on a 53-year-old owner of $21,721.
- You may also use the fixed annuitization method. For the above example, this method would produce a SEPP distribution of $21,617.

You can get a one-time Mulligan for a SEPP calculation. Rev. Rul. 2002-62 permits a one-time change in the calculation method used[17]. Thus, if the market made a significant change in the IRA value, or your facts and circumstances changed, you could make a one-time change from whatever method you used to another more favorable calculation.

Do not modify the SEPP stream once it is calculated. Modification means increasing, decreasing, stopping or transferring into or out of the SEPP IRA. You have to leave the IRA alone for a time period of the longer of 5 years or number of years to attain age 59 ½.

You also should know on SEPP that the calculation is done on a per-IRA basis. So if you were 53 and had a $1,000,000 IRA, but only needed about $21,721, you could split the IRA and take a SEPP on a $500,000 IRA and leave the other. You can have as many SEPP calculations of separate IRAs as you want. If you start a new SEPP calculation, the rule of 5 years or age 59 ½ time testing applies to each calculation.

All in all, the SEPP exception is a good way to access IRA money early if you need it. But it's like the mercury lights we used to have in the gym in school way back in the 60s: once you turn it on, you have to leave it on, for the longer of 5 years or age 59 ½.

Idea 26: Use a Qualified Plan or 403(b) to dodge RMDs. Traditional IRAs require RMDs to begin at age 70 ½. If you are over 70 ½ and still working at a company that you don't own 5% or more of, you can roll your Traditional IRA into a 401(k) or 403(b). You're not required to withdraw from those plans until after you retire. Remarkably, the IRS does not define 'retirement' anywhere. Probably getting a W-2 indicates you are not retired. This tip allows us to defer RMDs.

Idea 27: Use an IRA rollover to avoid 20% withholding on a Qualified Plan distribution. Qualified Retirement Plans (QRPs), like 401(k) plans, must withhold 20% on any distributions. So, if you had $50,000 in the plan and wanted to take it all out, the plan is required to withhold $10,000 ($50,000 x 20%). Suppose you had significant losses, like a Net Operating Loss on a business, or very large itemized deductions, you could avoid the withholding by rolling or transferring the QRP to an

IRA, then making an IRA distribution. You can elect to have no withholding on an IRA distribution.

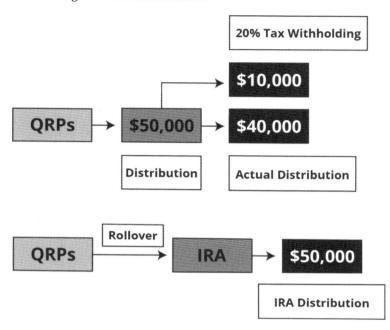

Idea 28: Make Roth contributions after age 70 ½. A Roth IRA has a variety of advantages, notably how it works with the age 70 ½ rule. The most notable age 70 ½ rule about a Roth IRA is that it is not subject to RMDs at age 70 ½. The second and lesser-known 70 ½ rule for a Roth IRA is that, unlike a Traditional IRA, you can contribute to a Roth IRA after age 70 ½. This is good news for someone over 70 ½ who either has earned income, or is married to someone with earned income. The general Roth strategy is to load them up and you can do that post age 70 ½ if one person in a couple has earned income.

Idea 29: Use the age 55 exemption from a Qualified Plan. There is a tax advantage for a Qualified Retirement Plan versus an IRA on taking distributions early. In an IRA (and a Qualified Plan), you may be subject to a penalty if you withdraw before age 59 ½. One useful exception is the Substantially Equal Periodic Payments (SEPP), or §72(t) exemption (See Idea 25). This can be applied to IRAs or Qualified Plans. Qualified Plans have another exception to the 10% early withdrawal penalty, which is when you take a withdrawal from a qualified plan upon separation from service and in the year you attain 55 or older. A couple of important points here: First, it is the year you attain 55, not that you actually have to be 55. So if you were born in December like me, you would have 11 months of being 54 that still count as age 55. The second point is frequently misread: You have to separate from service in that year that you attain 55 or older. So if you retire in the year you attain 54, this doesn't work. If you are 55 or older in the year you retire and take a withdrawal, it does. Taking the distribution in the year after you retire at age 54 won't work. This exception can be handy for retirees older than 55 and under 59 ½. Suppose Lucius is 58 and retires from X Corp. He has a $400,000 balance in his 401(k). He could take a withdrawal to hold him over to age 59 ½, say $25,000 and rollover the rest to his IRA. When he turns 59 ½, he could make withdrawals on his own terms, not subjecting himself to the restrictions of the SEPP.

Idea 30: Use the age 50 exemption if you are a police officer or firefighter. Note the above exemption of age 55 is modified for first-responders, primarily police officers and firefighters. If you are a first-responder and have separated from service in the same year of attaining the age of 50, taking a withdrawal from a pension plan (like an annuity withdrawal, 401(a) or a DROP plan) will not be subject to the 10% tax penalty.

Idea 31: Pay management fees on a regular IRA out of the IRA. For large Roth IRAs, it makes sense to pay management fees out of outside funds, just like it makes sense to pay the taxes on a Roth conversion from outside funds. Roth IRAs are tax-free and growing them as much as possible is the goal. On the other hand, regular IRAs are taxable creatures. As such, taking the management fee from the taxable money effectively makes the fee fully tax deductible. You can pay investment expenses out of your own pocket and build the IRA, but on a Traditional IRA this would only be a miscellaneous itemized deduction subject to the 2% AGI floor.

Here is a warning against taking this tip too far: Don't use your regular IRA to pay fees for other accounts, like taxable accounts or Roth IRAs. By doing that, you are running square into the risk of a prohibited transaction. Pay those fees from their respective accounts.

Idea 32: Buy actual Real Estate in your IRA. You can buy property such as a home or raw land in a self-directed IRA through IRA custodians that specialize in this market. On the surface, it makes sense that buying and selling real estate free of tax is a good idea, but the following must be considered before going forward:

- You lose many of the tax advantages of owning property. You cannot depreciate property in an IRA. So if the real estate has a building or other depreciable asset on it, you lose a tax deduction.
- Holding property long term in an IRA does not make much sense. Any gains on property held for more than one year are still generally treated as ordinary income when taken from the regular IRA as opposed to long term gain treatment. If you put real estate in a Roth IRA, the gain is tax-free, but long-term capital gains are still a tax advantage, being as low as 0% and as high as 20% or 23.8% if you add in potential net income tax.

- You and your relatives are barred from working on the property. No "sweat equity", or risk getting hit with tax evasion and/or prohibited transactions.
- All improvements must be hired out to an unrelated party.
- All expenses, renovations or upkeep must be paid for out of the IRA.
- If you plan to rent the property out you generally must hire a manager to find tenants.
- You will expect to pay cash for the home. Getting a mortgage is very difficult and can trigger a tax upon tax on that portion of the income attributable to the financed part of the transaction, called Unrelated Debt-Financed Income[18].
- If you have a loss, you cannot write that off. If you kept the property out of the IRA, you could.
- There are not many companies that handle these types of IRAs. The cost to start and to maintain can be very high.
- You or any family members cannot use the property for any personal benefits. You, your spouse or family members cannot buy the property from the IRA or sell property to the IRA. You must know and follow the Disqualified Persons Rules[19]. No family cottages in the IRAs.
- The IRA custodian must keep track of and report on deposits, withdrawals and year-end balances.

With all the rules and tax disadvantages, who should consider buying real estate in an IRA? A very experienced real estate investor who flips houses or raw land and the income earned is normally taxed as ordinary income (so think parking lots or farmland). The investor would need a large IRA (ideally a large Roth IRA) in order to pay for, and possibly upgrade and maintain the property. If using a contributory IRA, it would also make sense that the investor is currently in a high tax bracket now and expects to be in the same or lower tax bracket later. Finally, you must be very diligent in following the rules, or you will lose IRA status and there will be severe tax consequences, including the investment being treated as a distribution (if under 59 ½ an added 10% penalty) and the participant is subject to a 15% excise tax on the amount involved for each year, plus additional penalties accruing for each year before the IRS catches the violation.

Idea 33: Deduct the loss on your Roth. We know that one advantage to an IRA is tax deferral of investment gains and the advantage in a Roth is tax-free investment gains. However, there is an interesting advantage: You can deduct a loss, including a loss on IRAs and Roth IRAs. Not only that, the loss is deductible from ordinary income and not on a capital loss. It sounds weird that Roth gains are tax-free and losses can be deductible. Well, the rules show why this is very narrow in scope.

First, the rule applies to Traditional IRAs and Roth IRAs separately. In other words, you can deduct losses on your Roth IRAs or your Traditional IRAs, or both. However, and this is important, you have to close all of your Traditional or Roth IRAs. This means you have to knock off all gains and losses netted. Second, the loss is deducted as a miscellaneous itemized deduction. You may deduct the difference between the basis (what you paid) and the value. So, if you made total Roth contributions to all of your Roth IRAs of $20,000 and bought a terrible investment now worth $5,000, you could deduct $15,000. The deduction would go on your Schedule A as a miscellaneous Itemized deduction. You could only deduct the portion that all of certain itemized deductions were greater than 2% of your Adjusted Gross Income. This might include tax preparation fees and investment expenses. You can deduct a loss on a Roth, but only in limited circumstances. A better bet is not to make terrible investments.

Idea 34: The QLAC. The Qualified Longevity Annuity Contract (QLAC) isn't really a new type of annuity. It is simply a new tax treatment approved on July 1, 2014, by Internal Revenue Service, for types of annuities that are purchased in Traditional IRAs, 401(k)s and other approved retirement plans[20]. You put in a lump-sum up to 25% of your IRA or $125,000, whichever is less, fund in QLAC. The insurance company tells you today exactly how much fixed annuity income you will begin receiving in the future, regardless of how long you live. QLAC fund is excluded from your required minimum distribution (RMD) calculations, which could potentially lower your taxes. As an example, if you have a $600,000 Traditional IRA, you could fund a $125,000 QLAC (not $150,000) under the current rule. Your RMD would then be calculated on $475,000. There is no stock market or interest rate risk, therefore the principal is protected. QLACs allow you to defer as long as 15 years or to age 85. QLAC has no annual fees. Commission to agent is built into the product, which is very low when compared with fully-loaded variable or indexed annuities. Cost-of-living adjustment (COLA) can be attached to increase the annuity, if the carrier allows it.

Idea 35: Filing a 5329 to set the statute of limitations.
IRAs are tax favored accounts that are subject to many restrictions, which can translate to added risks in the form of tax penalties. Just to name a few: 6% penalty for excess contributions, 10% penalty for distributions prior to age 59 ½ (unless an exemption is applied) and a daunting 50% penalty if failed to take a Required Minimum Distribution (RMD).

Most people know that a statute of limitation runs three years starting the return due date or filing date whichever is earlier. Here is the terrifying truth: If you did not file Form 5329, (Additional Taxes on Qualified Plans and Other Tax-Favored Accounts) by attaching it to Form 1040 or separately, the clock of the three-year statute of limitation in regards to IRA penalty will not be set to start until when the error is detected. In 2011 case of *Robert K. and Joan L. Paschall v. Commissioner*[21], the Tax Court decided the Roth conversion the Paschall's did in 2000 was improper. The transaction is deemed as an IRA taxable distribution. The three-year statute of limitation for this unreported income expired. However, the IRS treated the conversion as an excess contribution to the Roth IRA. Since form 5329 was not filed, the statute of limitations clock wasn't set. The IRS was able to impose a 6% penalty annually on this excess contribution. Doing a conversion? File Form 5329 with your 1040.

Idea 36: Mind your beneficiaries. You should pay attention to the financial situation of your beneficiaries. For beneficiaries in the high tax bracket, leave them the Roth IRA, since the taxes have already been paid. For beneficiaries in a low tax bracket, leave them the Traditional IRA. If you want to leave an IRA to a charity, leave the charity a Traditional IRA. Be careful if you want to leave an IRA to <u>both</u> individuals and charities, because it could cause your individual beneficiaries to lose the stretch (see Idea 44) and accelerate taxes. You should also pay attention when leaving an IRA to a 'special needs' beneficiary. Naming the special needs individual as a beneficiary could cause them to lose government benefits. It is better to name the individual's Special Needs Trust as the beneficiary and not the individual directly. Finally, think about the individual you want to name as a beneficiary: Are they a credit risk? Is there potential for a divorce? Can they manage the IRA? In any of these instances you may want to consider an IRA Trust (see Ideas 3 and 4).

Idea 37: How to write a good beneficiary designation. A good beneficiary designation clearly states where your IRA will go after your death. You should name both primary and secondary beneficiaries. For married couples, the spouse is usually named as the primary beneficiary and the children as secondary or contingent beneficiaries. To name individual beneficiaries, give the complete legal name of each beneficiary. For multiple beneficiaries, you must also state the percentage of the IRA each will receive. For example, 50% to Jack Doe and 50% to Jill Doe. You can add *per stirpes* after the name of an individual beneficiary if you want that beneficiary's children to get the share if the beneficiary you named predeceases you. If you name a revocable trust as a beneficiary, you will need to give the name of the trust and the date the trust was created. Make sure your Revocable Trust has the correct language (see idea 48). If you name an IRA trust as a beneficiary, you would use the following designation: "name of trust, date trust created, FBO name of beneficiary". Typically, the custodian of the IRA

has a beneficiary designation form. If the custodian does not have a beneficiary form, you should give the custodian a written statement listing your beneficiaries.

 Idea 38: Leave your Traditional IRA to charity. For a taxable estate (e.g., above $10.68M per married couple or 5.43M per individual in 2015), the naming of a charity as a beneficiary has a double benefit: There are no income taxes to the charity and there are no estate taxes on the gift to the charity. If you had a taxable estate (which I fervently hope you do) and you have charitable intent, then leaving the IRA to the charity makes the most sense by a long shot. You save income taxes on the IRA and estate taxes. Obviously, a charitably minded donor would be best leaving the IRA to charity and other assets to a non-charity beneficiary. From a planning standpoint, it makes sense to segregate the portion you want to leave to a charity, into a separate IRA, to not confuse the IRA beneficiaries. In other words, if you want to leave $50,000 to charity, then segregate a $50,000 IRA and name the charity the beneficiary.

Idea 39: Leave your IRA to a Charitable Remainder Trust. You can leave an IRA to a Charitable Remainder Trust (CRT). A CRT provides income to an income beneficiary and a remainder interest to a charity. The income from the charity can be a fixed amount, in which case it's called a Charitable Remainder Annuity Trust (CRAT)[22], or a percentage of the Trust's income, where it is called a Charitable Remainder Unitrust (CRUT)[23].

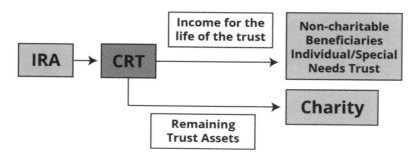

If the CRT meets the strict requirements of the code, it will provide an income to the beneficiary, plus an estate tax deduction to the estate for the charitable gift. This is ideal where an IRA owner wants to provide for their favorite charity and have some income to heirs, for a period up to 20 years. This can work out in a variety of circumstances, such as where there is an older beneficiary or a special needs beneficiary. In this case, the IRA is left to the CRT with the life beneficiary as a Special Needs Trust. The Special Needs Trust allows the disabled beneficiary to receive additional benefits above any governmental benefits, which otherwise might have been reduced or lost. The CRT also works well where you have a desire to leave a specific periodic amount to a group of beneficiaries.

 Idea 40: Leave your IRA to a Charitable Gift Annuity. A Charitable Gift Annuity provides a lifetime income to a beneficiary and the remainder to charity. The gift to the charity is deducted from the decedent's estate (based on its present value). The benefit to the charity is not subject to income taxes. This would work well where there is a taxable estate, older beneficiaries and a charitable intent.

 Idea 41: Don't leave your Roth to charity. As much as leaving a Traditional IRA to charity is a good idea, leaving your Roth to charity is not. Roth IRAs are tax-free and so are charities. You paid the tax on funds that went into the

Roth, whether via conversions or contributions. Use taxable IRAs or capital gains asset to fund charitable gifts. Leave the Roth to humans.

Idea 42: Don't try to convert an inherited IRA to a Roth. This is commented on and asked by a lot of people. But here's an easy answer: You can't convert an inherited IRA to a Roth because the law doesn't allow it[24]. So don't do it.

Idea 43: Title your Inherited IRA correctly. Inherited IRAs (as opposed to your IRA or a spousal IRA) must be titled correctly to show the IRA as being received from a decedent. Ed Slott suggests the following designation, which I agree with: "John Smith, IRA (deceased December 16th, 2014) F/B/O John Smith Jr., beneficiary". Remember that you cannot roll over an Inherited IRA to a Traditional IRA in your own name, nor can you convert it to a Roth (See Idea 42).

Idea 44: Stretch the benefit of the Inherited IRA. IRA beneficiary rules are complex. For non-spouse beneficiaries, a preferred method, tax-wise, is to 'stretch' the payout over the life expectancy of the beneficiary. This is done through separate accounts for each beneficiary, created by September 30th of the year following the IRA owner's death. It's important that an IRA bequest by that date be as percentages, not as dollars, and all to individuals. So it would be fine to leave an IRA to Huey, Dewy and Louie in equal shares (33⅓ %). It would not be fine to leave Huey $50,000 and Dewy and Louie 50% of the remainder. In that case, paying Huey before the 09/30 beginning date would be preferable. Likewise, if a charity was a partial beneficiary of an IRA (See Ideas 38-40), paying the charity earlier or using a separate IRA for the charity makes sense. In a 'stretch', we also want to name an alternate beneficiary to receive the RMDs the beneficiary would have taken.

Our basic 'stretch' rules for multiple beneficiaries:

- Name individuals as beneficiaries of the particular IRA you want to stretch.
- Establish a separate Inherited IRA account for each of the separate beneficiaries by September 30th and begin taking distributions (RMDs) by December 31st of the year following the owner's death.
- Name a contingent beneficiary on the Inherited IRA.

Idea 45: Asset protection tip, don't comingle rollovers and Traditional IRAs. According to federal bankruptcy law, Rollover IRAs have unlimited protections, while Contributory IRAs only have $1M of protection[25]. If you have both, it's probably not a good idea to comingle them.

Idea 46: Use an IRA to get special withdrawal treatments if under 59 ½. There are some special exemptions to the early withdrawal penalty that are only applicable to IRAs. These include:

- Health insurance premiums for the unemployed[26].
- Qualified higher education expenses[27].
- Qualified first-time homebuyer expenses[28].

You can use this for a younger person to buy a house (I did this with my daughter's IRA). You could also roll some money out of a qualified plan into an IRA and use the exceptions. So a younger person might roll over from their Qualified Plan to take advantage of the first-time homebuyer exception.

Idea 47: Roll over a Designated Roth Account (DRAC) to a Roth IRA. 401(k) plans and 403(b) plans can offer Designated Roth Accounts, or DRACs. These accounts can allow a significant building of tax-free money, much larger than a Contributory Roth, since the DRAC has the same limits as a conventional 401(k) or 403(b) plan. However, DRACs, for some perplexing reason, are subject to the Required Minimum Distribution (RMD) rules, whereas Roth IRAs are not. Accordingly, when you retire from a 401(k) or 403(b) with a DRAC, roll the DRAC into a Roth IRA so you have no Required Minimum Distribution. Be careful if you intend to take the money out of the Roth soon after the rollover: Both DRACs and Roth IRAs have a 5-year holding period for a qualified distribution. If you are close to the 5-year period but not over it, it may be better to wait.

Idea 48: If you name a trust as a beneficiary, make sure it has a see-through provision. Naming your Revocable Living Trust (not an IRA Trust, see Idea 4) as an IRA beneficiary, will allow tax deferred growth for your individual beneficiaries, if the trust has the correct see-through language. If your trust does have the correct language, the IRA will flow through the trust and will then be divided into separate Inherited IRAs, one for each individual beneficiary you named in your trust. The age used to calculate the Required Minimum Distributions for all of your beneficiaries will be the age of your oldest beneficiary. If you have already named your revocable trust as the beneficiary, you should check with either the attorney who drafted the trust or another estate planning attorney to make sure that the trust has been properly drafted to be named as the beneficiary of your IRA.

Idea 49: Use your Roth IRA as a college education savings tool. Many people do not have the financial resources to save enough for retirement and college for their child (ren). Often, people will add to college accounts and neglect their retirement savings. While it is noble to think of your children before yourself, you can actually do both at the same time. You can add $5,500 per year (or $6,500 if 50 years old or more) to a Roth, assuming you qualify under the income rules and another $5,500 (or $6,500 if 50 years old or more) for your spouse. Let's say you save the max for you and your spouse for 18 years, while under 50 years old, you would have $198,000 just in principal! That does not take into account that the amount you can contribute increases depending on the rate of inflation.

While a Roth IRA was meant for retirement by law, it has rules that make it a useful tool for college savings. First, with a Roth IRA you are able to take the principal out at any time with no penalty or tax! For qualified education expenses, you can take the principal out penalty and tax free, but the earnings are taxed as ordinary income. If your child does not go to college, gets a scholarship, joins the military or you are having financial hard times, you can access those funds for other reasons and possibly get financial aid for your children. There is a lot of flexibility. When you have limited resources, flexibility is important and provides some safety net for the family.

Another benefit of contributing to a Roth versus a 529 plan is the rule to decide eligibility to financial aid. Assets in an IRA or Roth IRA do not count towards calculating financial aid. Only when money is withdrawn from an IRA is it counted as the parents' income and against financial aid. Money in a 529 plan is counted against the financial aid calculation, although at a favorable rate, depending on whether the parent or grandparent owns the account. Money in an UGMA/UTMA counts as the student's asset. How these assets are counted has changed many times and probably will change again, but I would bet that retirement assets in the future will still count more favorably than education savings.

The moral of the story is that a Roth IRA gives you flexibility. Here is another example: Let's say your children are just about to start college and you have paid off all your debts and you now have ample income to pay for college! Why even touch the Roth? Now instead of having a bunch of money in a 529 plan that will have to be taken out, you have a huge IRA that you can use for retirement while keeping the favorable tax status.

Idea 50: Use the Roth IRA as an emergency fund account. Sounds weird but most young people just starting out in their career, have little savings and are not thinking of retirement. The idea of putting money into an account and not seeing it for 30-40 years is unthinkable. One of the first priorities in financial planning is having an emergency fund that you can access quickly. Most people think a bank account is the only option, but banks are not paying much interest right now. A Roth IRA is viewed as an account that cannot be accessed quickly, but that has changed. You can set up an electronic link to your Roth directly to your bank account and have those funds available in 1-2 business days. The principal is always available tax and penalty free.

The reason a Roth IRA makes sense is that an emergency fund is not always used. If you add to the Roth over several years and find your income has grown, then you can add to an emergency fund at the bank with any extra income. Now you have several years of Roth IRA contributions in your Roth IRA and an emergency fund. You have also gained a lot of flexibility in the process.

Conclusion. IRAs, both Traditional and Roth IRAs, are wonderful planning tools. They can allow tax savings, beneficiary protection and even the creation of a family dynasty. We thought the attached 50 ideas would be helpful to you, whether you are an IRA owner, a beneficiary of an IRA, or a professional advisor. At LJPR Financial Advisors, we like to take a big picture view: To look at the whole picture of how the IRA integrates with the tax plan and the estate plan. How the investments in the IRA correspond to the outside investments. If you would like information on managing an IRA, the tax planning aspects of IRAs or the estate planning consequences of IRAs, or if you'd like to experience a fiduciary, fee-only advisor, please feel free to contact us. We'll try to answer any questions you may have.

Endnotes

[1] *Alvan L. Bobrow et ux.*, 107 T.C.M. 1110 (2014)
[2] *Clark v. Rameker*, 134 S. Ct. 2242 (2014)
[3] IRS Single Life Expectancy Table
[4] Notice 2014-54, I.R.B. 2014-41
[5] I.R.C. §86(a)(2)
[6] I.R.C. §§408(d)(8)(A), 408(d)(8)(B)
[7] Distributions from Individual Retirement Arrangements (IRAs), Pub. 590-B
[8] IRS News Release IR-2014-99, I.R.B. 2014-18
[9] Form 8606, Nondeductible IRAs
[10] Form 5329, Additional Taxes on Qualified Plans (Including IRAs) and Other Tax-Favored Accounts
[11] I.R.C. §408A(d)(7)
[12] I.R.C. §408(d) (3); Treas. Reg. 1.408-8. Q&A 5(a)
[13] I.R.C. §401(a)(9)(B)(iv)(I); Treas. Reg. 1.401(a)(9)-3, Q&A 3(b)
[14] I.R.C. §401(a)(9)(C)
[15] IRS Uniform Lifetime Table
[16] I.R.C. §7520(a)(2)
[17] Rev. Rul. 2002-62, 2002-2 C.B. 710.
[18] I.R.C. §514(a)
[19] I.R.C. §4975(c)(1)
[20] Treas. Reg. 1.401(a)(9)-6
[21] *Robert K. Paschall,* 137 T.C. 8 (2011)
[22] I.R.C. §664(d)(1)
[23] I.R.C. §664(d)(2)
[24] I.R.C. §408(d)(3)(C)
[25] The Bankruptcy Code, 11 U.S.C. §522
[26] I.R.C.§72(t)(2)(D)
[27] I.R.C.§72(t)(2)(E)
[28] I.R.C.§72(t)(2)(F)

LJPR Financial Advisors
5480 Corporate Drive, #100
Troy, MI 48098
[p] 248 641-7400
ljpr.com